Lovers of the Deep-Fried Circle
Copyright © 2019 by Baruch Porras-Hernandez

Cover photograph by Mark McBeth // Used by permission

Author photograph by author

Cover design by Seth Pennington

All rights reserved. No part of this book may be reproduced or republished without written consent from the publisher, except by reviewers who may quote brief excerpts in connection with a review in a newspaper, magazine, or electronic publication; nor may any part of this book be reproduced, stored in a retrieval system, or transmitted in any form, or by any means be recorded without written consent of the publisher.

Sibling Rivalry Press, LLC
PO Box 26147
Little Rock, AR 72221

info@siblingrivalrypress.com

www.siblingrivalrypress.com

ISBN: 978-1-943977-61-1

By special invitation, this title is housed in the Rare Book and Special Collections Vault of the Library of Congress.

First Sibling Rivalry Press Edition, February 2019

LOVERS OF THE DEEP-FRIED CIRCLE

BARUCH PORRAS-HERNANDEZ

SIBLING RIVALRY PRESS
DISTURB / ENRAPTURE
LITTLE ROCK / ARKANSAS

for Wonder Dave

"... and there we are again and again
cause you and I will always be back then,
you and I will always be back then,
that's why
you and I will always be best friends ..."

"Time Adventure" by Rebecca Sugar

CONTENTS

Porque si lo pierdes   pierdes el camino / 7

Resting Gently on Her Unibrow / 8

Death Cry / 9

Dating Tips for Lonely Gay Men / 11

As a Gay Man It Is Good to Have Goals / 13

Dog.   Person. / 15

Unicorn on Fire / 16

Famous Inspirational Quotes
Frida Kahlo Did Not Say / 17

The Trees, They Hate the Birds the Most / 20

Glowing Marigolds / 22

The Sexual Fetishes of San Francisco / 27

Things I Have Failed At / 29

Thin, I Thin / 31

First Gentleman / 34

Oh the Places You Will Go, Fearing for Your Life
While People Do Drugs / 36

Lovers of the Deep-Fried Circle / 39

Love in the Time of Piñatas / 40

PORQUE SI LO PIERDES
PIERDES EL CAMINO

People ask me all the time,
You're Mexican, and gay, oh my gosh, what is that like?

I tell them it's like being a taco truck, covered in glitter
that plays Selena all the time, and gives great head.

Being Mexican and gay means I'm good at two things:
eating chorizo, and eating chorizo.

Look, just like any other gay man, I too
hear my parents crying in my head

every time I make love to a man, it's just in Spanish:
It sounds like this: Hijo, no! No lo hagas, hijo NO!
Porque? No seas gay! I normally respond
to the voices in my head:
Lo siento Mamá, Papá, me gusta el dick!

Being Mexican and gay is like being a piñata,
you're big, unapologetically covered in gorgeous beautiful colors.

The more fabulous, the more in danger you are
of being hit the face with a bat

but you still shake your stuff, you're brave,
shining as bright as you can as you soar through the air.

RESTING GENTLY ON HER UNIBROW

She had several self-portraits in which she painted
an object on her forehead.
If it was a small painting of her husband, it would be titled,
Thinking of Diego.
If the object was a skull, it would be titled,
Thinking of Death.

Oh Frida, if only I could be a small image on your forehead,
resting gently on your unibrow, with a small painting
on my forehead of a donut.

It would be titled, *Frida,*
Thinking of Chubby Mexican Immigrant,
Thinking of a Donut,
and at the top of the donut,
where the donut's forehead would be, between the sprinkles,
a small painting of Frida Kahlo,

and on her forehead, a small painting of me,
and on my forehead,
a small painting of a donut,
and so on, and so on, forever, and forever,
and forever.

DEATH CRY

I was in fourth grade
and obsessed with death.
My teacher, tired of me starting each day with—
*Why should I learn anything? We're all
just going to die, anyway.*—tells me
to take time to watch the leaves fall.
Says it would clear my mind.
Help give me some answers.

I tried it,
watching leaves fall.
All I saw were fucking leaves,

Falling.

So I started giving them
their own individual death cries.

No dear god! I had so much more to give!
A leaf would scream as it slowly
fell from a tree.

I regret nothing!

Goodbye, cruel world!

Celia, I never loved you!

I heard all the whisperings and kisses
between you and that leaf from the other branch.
I'll never forgive you!
With my last brown crinkly breath
I curse you!

I never liked making leaves crunch under my feet.

DATING TIPS FOR LONELY GAY MEN

When my friend is out on a date,
he begs me to text him things
he could say to make the date go better.

I used to say be yourself, be open to
fun and new experiences, and never lie.
But he never listened to me, and his dates
went to shit. Still he begged, saying
come on man, you're a writer, tell me
what to say. So I began texting him
words to woo boys to:

Tell him he is like apples, crisp and sweet,
you like apple juice, you wanna sit him on
the head of small boy, stab an arrow through him.
If that doesn't work, just whisper the word, "Anal."

Tell him he is the nuts on your coconut donut,
you want to part the walls of his jelly roll,
peel him like a fruit roll-up. If that doesn't work,
wink, hold his hand across the table, and whisper "Anal?"

Tell him you will never leave him even
if he gets evicted and loses his job and has
to get food stamps and can't go to brunch anymore
'cause the connection is all you need, love is free
and so is anal.

Tell him you're so into him you'd be willing
to listen to Katy Perry all day, especially during anal.

Tell him your skills include gently caressing
his balls in your mouth with your tongue
while simultaneously cutting you both
a piece of pie out of the fridge 'cause you're a
multitasking kinda man, so much so that
you'd be willing to try some
double pene-tra-Anal.

Tell him he is an island,
you are raindrops on the palm trees,
he is barefoot, you are sand between his toes,
he is a tropical blowjob, you swallow,
cough three times, slide a napkin
over to him on which you've written
the word "Anal."

Tell him you believe in gay rights,
our gay ancestors didn't die for our freedom
so you to have to wait till the second date
for some anal!

Tell him when he gets old,
you'll most likely leave him
for a 24-year-old toxic twink
who has a career in the tech industry
and already owns a house, but you two
can still be friends right?
and sometimes meet, for some anal?

Tell him he has nice eyes.

AS A GAY MAN IT IS GOOD TO HAVE GOALS

List of Goals Option One:
    Get the Macklemore haircut that
    everybody in fucking San Francisco fucking has.
    Lose 150 pounds.
    Keep beard.
    Get tats.
    Then only hang out
    quietly and mysteriously with
    other gay tatted-skinny-hipsterbeards.
    Stare off into space
    like baristas trying too hard to pretend not to care.

List of Goals Option Two:
    Lose 175 pounds. Get a spiky gay haircut with frosted tips.
    Wear nothing but shorts and polo shirts.
    Call all my male friends *bro*. Ignore all women.
    Only talk to men if we are talking about how to make money.
    Buy a giant house after displacing poor people. Never use it.
    Kick brown children off of public soccer fields.
    Slut-shame men who are in open relationships.
    Make fun of the word polyamory.
    Have anonymous sex at the gym.
    Go to Burning Man, ridicule people who can't afford to go.
    Talk about how much I like HBO's *Looking*,
    people should really give it another chance.
    Post pictures of myself at pool parties
    surrounded only by gay men that look exactly like me,
    staring off into space, like a poodle
    that has eaten too much dog food.

List of Goals Option Three:
    Lose all the weight, all of it.
    Stop using deodorant.
    Stop using toilet paper 'cause it kills trees.
    Let 20-year-olds live in my house
    but only if I can fuck them.
    Have orgies, dye my hair purple and green,
    rename myself Acorn Thistle,
    eat so much kale that I can't move,
    stare off into space like a baby
    farting itself to sleep.

List of Goals Latino Edition:
    Lose 50 pounds. Buy more hair products.
    Tan on the beaches of Brazil.
    Magically get my accent back.
    Open a chain of Mexican restaurants.
    Buy my parents a house, each.
    Fund all of the quinceañeras.
    Follow Ricky Martin on Twitter.
    Become friends with Ricky Martin.
    Seduce, make love to him, break his heart, then
    leave Ricky Martin!
    Ricky Martin writes a new bunch of love songs to me.
    They teach the world to love after heartbreak,
    the only way a powerful, gay Latino man can.
    As I listen to them in my house in the Hamptons,
    I eat a bowl of cereal, staring off into space
    like María Félix when she was bored out of her mind,
    covered in jewels.

DOG. PERSON.

It would probably run away, if I had a dog.
Not 'cause I'm mean or bad with dogs. I think
it would just get bored. Notice I'm not into it
playing, running, doing things, and the dog,
with my luck, would not like to fetch. If it's at all
like me, it would question everything. Be too
afraid to even hump a leg, or bite anything.
The silence between us would be unbearably
maddeningly, uncomfortable. *Can I pet your
dog?* people would ask. I would ask, *why?
Why do you want to touch an animal you don't
know?* The dog would also question this,
we would frown at people together.
Until the dog would leave me a note:
*Woof, woof, woof woof, woof woof,
woof woof woof, woof woof, woof
woof woof, woof woof woof woof woof
woof   woof woof woof, woof, woof,
woof woof woof woof, woof.*
Translation:
*Thank you I guess for your efforts, human.
I am leaving to go search for something
interesting to do with the rest of my short
dog life. Not that there is anything
interesting in this world so I guess
as a dog I will just wait to die.
I puked behind the couch. Forgive me.
Goodbye.*

UNICORN ON FIRE

One night
I sat in my room wondering
whether or not I should kill myself
for being gay. I didn't want to make it past sixteen.

Then my wall exploded.
A red, flaming unicorn
galloped into my room and said
SNAP THE FUCK OUT OF IT!
THERE'S NOTHING WRONG WITH YOU!!
I am a creature just like you! Mysterious! Fabulous! Pure!
Except you get to walk around the land of the living!
So stop being a little brat and LIVE YOUR LIFE!

Snap.

He disappeared.
My curtains and my room no longer on fire,
I finished my homework
and went back to masturbating to images
of Tom Cruise from the movie *Legend*.

FAMOUS INSPIRATIONAL QUOTES
FRIDA KAHLO DID NOT SAY

"I hope that in the future white women will put my face on T-shirts and make money with them. 'Cause I kinda do like capitalism it's like not even that bad y'all."
— Frida Kahlo

"In the future if I play my cards right people will make quilts with my face and some sugar skulls on it. That totally says badass radical socialist to me."
— Frida Kahlo

"Man I hope that someday in the future, people will say that there is no more appropriate way to celebrate my beautiful work and fascinating life as a feminist icon and painter than with unique hand-crafted wearable art pieces."
— Frida Kahlo

"I drank to drown my sorrows,
but the damned things learned to swim.
May they live on, hand-painted onto decorative
pencil skirts that come in all sizes."
— Frida Kahlo

"I don't paint my dreams. I paint my reality,
which I hope one day lives on in sock form,
with my face on some socks, and just when people feel
that socks are not enough may my reality be represented

in knee-high stockings, so that my 'unique' look can
help people feel sexy when they wear socks...
with my face on them,
but anyway, people, it is the 1930s in Mexico,
who wants to do the Charleston and get some enchiladas?"
— Frida Kahlo

"Make me into a finger puppet!"
— Frida Kahlo

"God I hope my picture hangs in Mexican taquerias
all over the U.S. some day.
Oh, I better catch my trolley."
— Frida Kahlo

"Dude, I hope someone someday captures the rebellious courage
with which I explored the vast spectrum of my sexuality
in a time when it was considered horrifically obscene and unheard
of in my country, especially for a woman, by painting my face
on a durable, mesh tote bag. A girl can dream."
— Frida Kahlo

"May white women masturbate to my suffering
for years to come!"
— Frida Kahlo

"Thank goodness it's Fri DAY!, get it? ... get it?
You get it!"
— Frida Kahlo

"May all of my deep sensual connections that I make
with my several lovers live on
in the future through the poetry
written by privileged, capitalist, upper-middle class
white millennials who have never traveled to Mexico,
but they will get me, I'm sure they will,
they will totally get me. Time to go do some shots
with my boo Trotsky, he's so Trots-cray!
#dickmatized #hereigoagain #mividaloca #puteria
#yolo #liveyourtruth #gettinthattrotD"

— Frida Kahlo

THE TREES, THEY HATE THE BIRDS THE MOST

No one knows this, but the trees are all assholes.
Huge, hateful, bitter assholes, all of them, and since
they can't move, they hate everyone and everything
that does. The trees have the ability to talk to each
other, but all they do is sit around talking smack.
Saying hateful things about women and fat boys.
If the trees could vote they would
vote against marriage equality.

The trees don't give a fuck about your dog.

The trees think you're a pathetic moron.
This world is wasted on you! they say as you walk by.
She doesn't really love you! they say as you carve
your girlfriend's name on to their skin.
The trees hate squirrels, chipmunks,
and birds. They hate birds the most.
Fuck you, bird! they say whenever a bird flies by.

I hope they all die, a tree says as a bird
makes a nest in a small hole in its trunk.
There is this one tree, that once a year
has nearly 45 nests within its branches.
It wants to commit suicide. Prays every day
that lightning will strike it so it can burn to the ground.

The trees remember a time before humans,
when a tree could just watch bears fuck in peace.
The oldest ones are patient, are willing to wait,
know that the walking bloody bags of bacteria
will eventually destroy themselves and give the earth
BACK TO THE TREES WHERE IT BELONGS!

But until then, the trees will continue to be dicks,
and make jokes about your mother.

They fucking hate your mother.

GLOWING MARIGOLDS

My phone rings and the words on the screen say Frida Kahlo, which is odd, because I don't have anybody on my phone with the name Frida Kahlo. Also, the real Frida Kahlo is dead. I answer anyway, and a voice on the phone says *Baruch, soy yo.*

Yo, quién? I ask. *Frida Kahlo, cabrón. I'm going to come visit you in San Francisco. It's been a while, and I'd like to pay my respects before it disappears. Light a candle next to an image of me, and I'll be on my way.*

I look around my bedroom. I don't have the heart to tell her that I'm the only artist in San Francisco without a plethora of Frida memorabilia in my room.

Sure! I say.

I need you to be my guide, I want to take a stroll in the Mission, maybe meet some of the white women who can't stop talking about me.

Sale y vale, I say, and the conversation ends.

I look all over my apartment and cannot find a picture of her, so I go into my roommate's room. My roommate is a lovely white lady, so I know she'll have a bunch of Frida stuff. In her room I find a poster of Frida, a blanket with Frida's face on it, a Frida marionette, a Frida finger puppet, a coloring book, and in her closet I find several skirts and socks and even panties with Frida's face on them. I decide that these images are not appropriate so I go back to my room. I search through my closet and find a paper bag from the Frida Kahlo exhibit that the SFMOMA did some years back with one of her self-portraits on it that I took from the gift shop. I tack it to my wall, light a Walgreen's scented candle in front of it, and Frida Kahlo shows up at my doorstep in the Mission by the time the sun rises.

You're wearing a hoodie? And sweatpants? I say walking down South Van Ness with her.

I wanted to be comfy. Frida looks around. *It's been a long trip. What do people eat around here?*

I tell her about burritos. I describe them in detail. She gets a little frown and says, *Gross.*

I say, *I know. When I got to this country, I thought the same thing, but they're good!* She doesn't agree. So I take her to Yamo instead, the hole-in-the-wall Burmese place on 18th. Frida loves the food and loves the ladies that work there. We finish, and she says, *Take me to the murals.*

As we walk I ask her if this is her first time in the Mission since she died.

Yes. The dead never visit San Francisco anymore.

Why? I ask.

It has become incredibly ... unwelcoming, she says.

I know, I say.

And we have better things to do. She smiles.

I show her all the new murals. She takes her time at every one. When we are done at Balmy Alley, the parade starts. A large procession full of mostly white folks come walking down 24th Street, all with white skulls painted on their faces. You can tell a few of them are taking it seriously, but most of the people are only there for the party.

Frida smiles at first, then looks perplexed. We walk alongside one of them, an attractive white young man completely dressed up as a skeleton from head to toe.

I ask him, *Hey man, what's this all about?*

He was drunk. *Dude, this is Mexican Halloween, man! Get into it!*

Frida snorts, *That's cute.*

The hipster gets scared for a second. *Who said that?*

Frida says, *Watch this*, to me, and lets him see her.

I said that, hi! She waves.

The hipster stares blankly at her, confused.

Oh, I forgot! she says, and transforms:

      a vibrant   flowing deep blue skirt,
screaming bright white huipil   blood red rebozo
woven to the braids of her hair   glowing marigolds

Now a glorious shining image of one of her paintings, all the hipsters recognize her right away. The whole parade comes to a halt. A white woman with voice shaking points to her and screams *It's Frida Kahlo!* All of the hipsters fall to their knees and begin to weep. They scream, *It is! It is her!*, all take out their iPhones, and begin to take pictures of her. Frida and I of course strike several poses. But then the hipsters keep crying, screaming, and get up to run towards us.

Frida says, *Follow me.* She starts running, so I start running.

You can run? I ask her as we run.

She frowns at me and says, *I'm dead, remember? I can do whatever I want.*

We lead the hipsters in a chase around the Mission. As we run, more hipsters join the screaming crowd. She leads them into an alley that dead ends at a large white wall. With nowhere to run, Frida and I look at the hipsters running towards us. They come upon us, like an avalanche, an unstoppable force, like a train that will not stop, like a Google bus that will not stop.

I think to myself, *Well, this is fitting, I'm going to die trampled to death by hipsters in the Mission.* Somehow it makes sense. Then, right as they are about to crash into us, Frida claps her hands and suddenly there is an explosion of sparks and glitter and smoke, and all of them disappear.

When the smoke rises, I see that all of the hipsters are now in a new mural on the large wall. They hold smartphones, coffee cups, money, laptops. Their faces are painted with white skulls. Frida laughs, lights a cigarette. Mexicans calmly come out of nowhere, stand in front of the mural, take out their flip phones or shitty disposable cameras and start taking pictures, then more pictures, and more pictures.

She sees my worried look. *Relax! They'll be fine tomorrow.*

Oh, cool. I say. *Some of my best friends are white.*

Frida smiles, takes a drag, and blows the smoke towards me. *Time for me to go*, she says. *I got a date with a bridge, feliz Día de Muertos.*

THE SEXUAL FETISHES OF SAN FRANCISCO

Douchebaggeophilia: sexual fetish for men in their 20s who work in startups funded by their daddies' money, already own a house, and have an undeserved sense of accomplishment.

Vinyasflophilia: sexual fetish for white women with dread locks who are usually wearing Rasta knit hats and Mexican folkloric skirts, and who have tattoos of Africa but have never left the U.S.

iPhonobroglassonica: sexual arousal from rubbing your genitals on broken iPhone screens.

Espressophilia: sexual need to ejaculate on latte art, but only when it's fair trade!

Debicardcosis: masturbating at the bank upon the realization that your checking account has more than four-hundred dollars in it, and you got to celebrate!

Hipstergentrificosis: sexual fetish for murals painted by Mexicans, and burritos made by Mexicans, but the need to not have to look at or deal with Mexicans.

Transportafantanism: when your pussy gets soooo wet, so wet! Because you actually got somewhere on time using San Francisco's abysmal public transportation!

I'mnotracistbutophilia: white men who are only attracted to Asian women but won't step foot in Chinatown cause they're scared of it.

Then there are the weird ones:

Nebulophiles: people aroused by the fog.

Avisodomy: sex with birds.

Dacryphilia: when one is aroused by tears or sobbing of others.

Whitefragiliophilia: when one is aroused by the tears or sobbing of white people.

Then there's my favorite:

Tacodonutrucomanosis: only being able to reach orgasm while on a taco truck speeding out of control that is on fire, while eating jelly donuts, but now knowing where the jelly donuts came from, then realizing that the jelly donuts don't have jelly in them, leading to severe panic attacks, but there is a cliff ahead, no brakes, the steering wheel is broken, and the jelly donuts are jelly-less, JELLY–LESS!

And lastly:

Sickofthisshit-a-ditus: when you're so sick of this shit that you just leave everything and go on walking and walking forever until you truly actually reach the end of the world, then jump off, arms wide open, open mouth, breathing in, and in, and in.

THINGS I HAVE FAILED AT

Being straight.

Learning about credit scores
and why the fuck they should matter.
Not running away when I was a kid.
Running away when I was a kid.
I always found my way back   or they found me.

Not lying at least once every day.
No, they're not terrible lies ... maybe.

Doing the right thing.

Killing myself.

Not drinking. AA.
The other twelve-step programs I've joined
that I won't mention because, whatever,
anonymous for a reason, right?

Being a good brother. Being a good son.
Being a good boyfriend.

Being a good friend. Being good to myself.
Being a good bottom.
Basketball.

Going to U.C. Berkeley. Sorry Dad.
Being Mexican. According to some Mexicans
I've been doing it wrong
for the past 32 years.

That is a lie. It's 35 years.

Having a savings account. Being Gay.
Technology. Acquiring property.
Knowing the correct meaning of words.
Grammar. Spelling. Monogamy.

Being in a band. Blogging. Not using deodorant.
Being a vegetarian. Being a vegan.
Being a raw vegan.

Catholicism. Atheism. Being Goth.
That one hurt. I really wanted to be Goth.

Learning French. Forgiving myself. Pushing myself.

Making sense of why I'm here.
Breaking through the walls of reality
in search of other realms or planes of existence
beyond comprehension
of my human understanding.

Growing up.

THIN, I THIN

When I lose weight, all of my lovers will leave me.
Those chubby chasers love the fat boy holding
the skinny boy trapped inside, but, oh! But, oh!
The pictures posted all over Facebook, of just
me, doing things, thin!

My mother will finally stop worrying about me.
She'll take down all the fat pictures of me off of
the fridge, call all of her friends, tell them she
finally has her son back!

When I lose weight
I'll be one of those, YES-park people!
YES-beach people! You're having a pool party?
YES! INVITE ME-kind-o-people!
I'll say things like, *You're right, it is pretty hot,
I should take my shirt off.*
No, I'm not afraid, I'm thin now!

Bathhouses, HERE I COME!

Sex clubs, WATCH OUT!

Nude beaches, nude art modeling,
nude house cleaning, I'll do it! Nude!
Nude! Nude! Nude! Nude! Nude!
     Nude, baby!

I'll take my clothes off every time I perform.
My art will be me, doing random things, naked.

I'll take needles ... and move them
from one pile of needles ... to ...
another pile of needles!
It will be art, and interesting, 'cause I'll be naked and
thiiiiiiiiiiiiiiiiiiiiiiiiiiiiiiiiiiiiiiiiiiiiiiiiiiinnnnn!
THIIIIIIIIIIIIIIIIIIIIIIIIIIIIN!!!! Thin, thin
Thin, think of all the parties I'll get invited to!
My thin queer friends and I will stand together
at the thin, gay,
> faerie,
>
> queer,
>
> radical,
>
> vegan
>
> gathering/sex party
>
> /dance party
>
> /craft-making THIN potluck
>
>> occupy-THIN movement!

We'll paint our faces white, draw skeletons
on them, march around holding hands.
It will be a flaco Día de los Muertos!
People won't be able to tell which one is me
and neither will I—thin, I thin, I mean, I think?

When I have sex, I won't know what to do
with all that space between my chest and my legs.
I'll let men touch my stomach, I'll keep the
motherfuckin' lights on!

One night after fucking all the thin men
and the thin men are sleeping (there's a lot of them
but they fit in my bed, since they're so thin!)
I'll sit, with my knees folded to my chest and
my arms around them. I'll marvel at my new ability
to sit in a way I have never been able to do.
I'll look out my window still holding my
thin knees, waiting for the skinny sun to rise
so it can come through my window
over to my ear to whisper all the secrets of life
it only whispers to skinny people
AT THIN DAWN!

FIRST GENTLEMAN

It's a good thing   I don' t have
          a nice ass   'cause it would be
the busiest ass on the street!
Putting in the long man hours to get me the manpower
to get what I want. Eventually landing me a sugar daddy
so I can play hubby all day, babysit the adopt-a-kids and
mandatory dog while I read Oprah's magazine,
sipping a latte at an expensive coffee shop
as the hubby fucks a 20-year-old European boy
while on a business trip he will later tell me about
while we watch *RuPaul's Drag Race* before going to bed
in our gigantic California king-size bed that is so big
we never have to rub up against each other ever again.

It's a good thing I don't have a nice ass,
cause it would be a dangerous piece of ass
that would always get me into trouble! Start distracting
the young-adult sons and hot-bod dads in the neighborhood!
Jealous hubby would start to cut my allowance in half,
accuse me of fucking Alessandro the Gardner, so to piss him off
I actually do start fucking Alessandro the Gardner.
Alessandro tries to leave his wife and kids for me
and I say, "No Alessandro, stay with Juanita!
You need to be strong and work hard
for Paco and Manuelita and Estevie,
Forget me, but most importantly
forget this ass!"

If I had a nice ass, my ass would be famous.
I would take advantage of how gay men are ass-obsessed
and take my ass across towns, across cities, all the way to the
beds of the men who control the world.
Eventually these powerful men would make me a diplomat.
My time as a diplomat would make me famous.
I would end up on *Oprah* on an episode
where she interviews powerful gay men.
The first good-looking, openly gay senator who is
also there asks me out to dinner because of this ass.
I say yes, and in four years, end up married to the first ever
openly gay president of the United States!
As First Gentleman of the country,
I begin a world tour of peace
                that pisses everybody off
and gets certain fuckheads in our shit country
angry that there is a gay dude as their leader.
Not willing to live in a world where gay men can be leaders.
the dumbfuck homophobes in the U.S.
start attacking other countries. That leads to conflict and war.
Eventually everybody launches their nukes,
making everybody kiss their butts goodbye
as the world ends
and my husband the President holds me close.
Before the fire wall of nuclear backlash incinerates us,
he says, "I will always love you..."
All that'll go through my mind is,
"Damn,
I should have been born with a normal ass."

OH THE PLACES YOU WILL GO, FEARING FOR YOUR LIFE WHILE PEOPLE DO DRUGS

Tiny poems inspired by riding the buses of San Francisco aka Muni

San Francisco! Richest
city in the West! Muni
still a pile of CRAP!

Rolling up, rolling down
Gatorade bottle full of pee
Metaphor for life on the 33

Young man stretching
to reach the pole, showing me his abs
killing me softly

Meth head on the five
opens broken laptop:
Driver, what's the Wi-Fi?

★   ★   ★

The 49, like the man who
puked on you during sex
then asked to spend the night

The 14, the cute bus boy
who stole your wallet
and your heart

The 24, a room full of
gay white men screaming
YAAAAAAAS!!, forever.

*   *   *

Bees in my eyes!
screamed the crackhead
drooling on the 12

Who needs deodorant!?!?!
screamed the teenagers
on all the buses

I make a lot of money!!!
screamed the douchey techie
on the 44 O'Shaughnessy

Hey don't sit there,
I peed, said the old lady
smiling on the 43

*   *   *

Muni, first place you saw
two men holding hands
making you feel less alone

Two old men talk about
how the city has changed
both agree, still beautiful!

Nighttime, old gay guy
tells me, "that's the house where I
lost Fred," then gets quiet

One day, we will all be ghosts
missing how it feels
to be on a bus, going home

One day, I will be a ghost
riding the bus, checking out
all the men's butts

★   ★   ★

Two bums knife fight
driver pulls over to eat tuna salad
calmly and watch

Racist old lady wants my
seat in the back because black teenagers
in the front scare her
my answer was "No, bitch."

LOVERS OF THE DEEP-FRIED CIRCLE

I love donuts.

They are like love:
        sweet
      fluffy
       sexy
          bad for you!
Sexy sugar holes that
    remind me of three wonderful things
        like
           mouths

            buttholes

            and glory holes.

LOVE IN THE TIME OF PIÑATAS

the white piñatas were always   shining   glittery
all of them with some silver here or there   never got beat
always on display   always   like disco balls   turning
up in the air   showroom models and   I was always
       the biggest puta piñata in the room
              lime greens concha pinks
A terrible combination
says one of the white piñatas from above,
FUCK YOU BITCH! I say. *Fuck you!*
I was made with love!
watch it   white piñata   watch it   I say
these points are sharp as fuck!
Yeah don't fuck with her! the Dora piñata would say
she got my back   she an explorer and shit
she is how we got the fuck out of there and shit
the Selena piñata came too   and so did Diego   and so did
Speedy Gonzales and that old Chilindrina piñata and el Chavo
too no one was gonna fuck with us   we ran from the
car accessories/cleaning supplies and piñata store we were at
thought we were goners but we were free   fuck
we even brought the white piñatas too
'cause we ain't cruel   freedom is for everybody
but the streets are fucked and people love to fucking kill us
but then but then   thank god
this fat chubby Mexicano gayhomosexual found us
and gracias church of the holy fuck this gay
chubby Mexican doesn't hurt his piñatas!

      he lets 'em live   forever

his house a piñata sanctuary!   his house a piñata paradise!
we up in his living room we up in his bedroom
the kitchen   the closets   the halls
we all over the damn place and we been having fun too
I've been a damn slut and it's been a piñatas orgy
been making out with a Batman piñata for three days
rubbing up against the Hulk piñata   sticking my peaks into
the rainbow unicorn in the corner   we all sweet as fuck
we all full of candy   the best part is he sold those white piñatas
to some fancy bitch from a place called the Marina and they gone!
we don't miss those white piñatas one bit!
some human girl came in the other day said, *hey aren't you*
supposed to beat these things? Aren't you supposed to
rip them apart and eat their candy?
the fat chubby Mexican kicked her out his house!   good!
      I like him   but I'm nervous

I'm still the fattest piñata in the room

still take up so much space

not shaped like one of these cool cartoon motherfuckers
even that round soccer-ball shaped cabrón
takes up less space than me
the chubby Mexican hugs us though   tells us we're safe
but I can tell he's sad   sees his friends move away
sees people getting shot and killed on the news
fuck not even humans in this world are safe

Piñata Dora wakes me up in the night
says we need to leave—*but here we're safe!* I tell her
she says, *we got a mission let's go, we're taking everyone!*
we leave the chubby Mexican a gift each
    a Gansito
    a Bubu Lubu   a Duvalín
    mango paleta covered in chile
        gomitas
  chocolate pelota filled with rompope
  something nice   to remember us by

we hit the road   the mermaid piñata
on the car piñata's back   Spiderman piñata
and Wolverine piñata   and Power Ranger piñata
walking next to Belle and Elsa Chilindrina
with El Chapulín at the head next to Dora and Diego
Batman holds on to one of my bright pink spikes
he says, *you're so big and gorgeous
and beautiful* and I say, *I know! Kiss me some more!*
we carry scissors and knives   and screwdrivers
Dora leads us to a store full of Donald Trump piñatas
I say, *No! they may be Donald Trump piñatas
but they still piñatas   we do not fuck with our kind no!
I won't do it!*   *We gotta do it!* Dora says
*In the ancient times   when we
were just brown heavy clay
they decorated us with feathers
ribbons of actual gold   shattered us
on the steps of Huitzilopochtli temples*

to symbolize a warrior's sacrifice
these Trump piñatas   it's time
for sacrifice—
NOOOO! I scream
Hey, says one of the Trump piñatas through the glass. *Hey, you're a whore, you're ugly and*
fat SAD!
I turn to Dora. *Okay do it*
but I won't take part.

I grab Batman piñata, split
walk into the night
away from the Mission knowing there are
people ready to break us beat us to a pulp
but no one bats an eye   no one gives a shit
it starts to rain   our paper gets wet   mushy
our insides begin to melt   we fall on the ground
ready to fucking leave it all   when
a light appears   I look up and there before
us are   500 glowing hummingbirds
in the shape of a gigantic being   its giant
glowing hands   reaching out to us made
of cosmic   little fucking   speedy   flapping
beautiful as fuck birds   I feel   less like melting
and more like   glowing   glowing   so much
it was like singing   like   I was   made of voices
and Batman too looks as surprised
and shocked as I am but then
we are in the black sky   and then we are

in space   so many   stars
my   soul   becomes a thousand fucking stars
and   I   finally   finally   shine!
brighter than all the white piñatas
but I am still pink as fuck   still green
but so shiny   so shiny   I twirl
like fucking crazy   like   the fucking
BIGGEST   DISCO BALL
IN   THE   MOTHER
FUCKING WORLD!!!

GRATITUDE

A very special thank you to Na'amen Gobert Tilahun.

Thank you to Ash Fisher, Miah Jeffra, Christina Ortega, Lark Omura, Zoe Young, Danae Barnes, and Joe Wadlington for reading early drafts of this chapbook.

Thank you to Eugenia Chen, Tara Ramproot and Muni Diaries, Cassandra Dallet, MK Chavez, Judith Tannenbaum, Carrie Gocker, Matthew Beld, Sina Grace, and a very special thank you to Matthew James Decoster, Kevin Seaman, Bryan Borland and Sibling Rivalry Press, Evan Karp, Michelle Tea, Juliana Delgado Lopera, Virgie Tovar, Marga Gomez, Siouxsie Oki, Yo Ann Martinez and everyone at KQED, Dhaya Lakshminarayanan, Meliza Banales, Tony Valenzuela, everyone at Lambda Literary Foundation, everyone at *Foglifter*, Jyoti Arvey, Marcus Ewert, Alvin Orlof and everyone at Dog Eared Books Castro, Sarah Guerra, Anastacia Powers Cuellar and everyone at Brava Theatre, Pam Pennington and everyone at the Queer Cultural Center, and KB Tuffy Boyce with Queer Rebels for always supporting my writing.

ABOUT BARUCH PORRAS-HERNANDEZ

Baruch Porras-Hernandez is a two-time winner of *Literary Death Match*, a regular host of poetry shows for KQED, and was named a Writer to Watch in 2016 by *7x7 Magazine*. His poetry can be found in several anthologies and journals such as Write Bloody Publishing's *Aim for the Head*, *The Tusk*, *Foglifter*, *Assaracus*, and many more. He has been an artist-in-residence at The Ground Floor at Berkeley Rep, a Lambda Literary Fellow in Poetry and in Playwriting, and was a Spoken Word resident artist at the Banff Center for the Arts in Canada. He is a recipient of grants from the San Francisco Arts Commission, Creative Work Fund, and Galería de la Raza. As a writer he has performed all over the place—NYC, LA, DC, parts of Canada, from *The Moth* to drag cabarets, from fancy universities to dark, damp caves. He was born in Mexico and lives in San Francisco.

ABOUT SIBLING RIVALRY PRESS

Sibling Rivalry Press is an independent press based in Little Rock, Arkansas. It is a sponsored project of Fractured Atlas, a nonprofit arts service organization. Contributions to support the operations of Sibling Rivalry Press are tax-deductible to the extent permitted by law, and your donations will directly assist in the publication of work that disturbs and enraptures. To contribute to the publication of more books like this one, please visit our website and click *donate*.

Sibling Rivalry Press gratefully acknowledges the following donors, without whom this book would not be possible:

Tony Taylor	Russell Bunge
Mollie Lacy	Joe Pan & Brooklyn Arts Press
Karline Tierney	Carl Lavigne
Maureen Seaton	Karen Hayes
Travis Lau	J. Andrew Goodman
Michael Broder & Indolent Books	Diane Greene
Robert Petersen	W. Stephen Breedlove
Jennifer Armour	Ed Madden
Alana Smoot	Rob Jacques
Paul Romero	Erik Schuckers
Julie R. Enszer	Sugar le Fae
Clayton Blackstock	John Bateman
Tess Wilmans-Higgins & Jeff Higgins	Elizabeth Ahl
Sarah Browning	Risa Denenberg
Tina Bradley	Ron Mohring & Seven Kitchens Press
Kai Coggin	Guy Choate & Argenta Reading Series
Queer Arts Arkansas	Guy Traiber
Jim Cory	Don Cellini
Craig Cotter	John Bateman
Hugh Tipping	Gustavo Hernandez
Mark Ward	Anonymous (12)

www.ingramcontent.com/pod-product-compliance
Lightning Source LLC
Chambersburg PA
CBHW051704040426
42446CB00009B/1301